2ND E[illegible]

*Concise Overview of*

# BUSINESS VALUATION

## *of Small and Midsize Private Companies*

*For Business Owners, Managers and Professionals Who Advise Them*

2ND EDITION

*Concise Overview of*

# BUSINESS VALUATION

## *of Small and Midsize Private Companies*

*For Business Owners, Managers and Professionals Who Advise Them*

DAVID L. PERKINS, JR.

**D. L. PERKINS, LLC.**
7010 S. Yale, Suite 120
Tulsa, OK 74136
800-634-0605
Fax: 918-493-4924
www.DLPerkins.com



This Report is intended to provide general information about the subject matter covered. It is sold and distributed with the understanding that the publisher, author and any distributor are not engaged in rendering legal, accounting, tax, insurance, or other professional services or advice. If legal advice or other expert assistance is required, the services of a competent professional should be sought.

ISBN # 0-9744172-1-1

Printed in the United States of America
1 2 3 4 5 2006 2007 2008 2009

*This book is dedicated to my father,*
***David Lindsay Perkins,***
*who stepped out of corporate life with courage,*
*at a young age, to "make it on his own"*
*and achieve success for himself and his family.*
*He provided well for us – both financially*
*and by his example.*

# Table of Contents

# Executive Summary

This publication provides a brief, honest, but thorough overview of valuation of private businesses. It is written for the business person who wants to understand the basic concepts of how private companies are valued. In the effort to be brief, the author has taken liberties, based on his experience, to "cut to the chase," if you will, and provide the reader with the essentials.

But the reader should not mistake brevity for simplicity. Many concepts are covered herein, some difficult to fully comprehend. The reader should not attempt to absorb the content in a single sitting but rather start at the beginning and then pause as long as needed at each section until the concept covered is grasped.

Armed with a working knowledge of business valuation, the reader will be able to make better financial decisions for himself or herself and will be able to assist others in doing the same. He or she will be able to accurately assess investment opportunities and negotiate more effectively. If knowledge is power, and if wealth attainment is the goal, then the subject matter covered herein will provide wealth-building power possessed by only a precious few.

# About the Author

David L. Perkins, Jr. is one of the leading experts in the United States on the purchase, sale and valuation of private companies. He has extensive formal training in business valuation; has personally consulted on more than 100 business purchase and sale transactions; has bought and sold companies for his own account; and holds various private and public investments. His 10-office consulting firm, Vercor (www.VercorAdvisor.com), is the leading merger and acquisitions advisory firm serving private companies with $5 million plus in annual revenues. Vercor's headquarters are in Atlanta.

Mr. Perkins is an award-winning writer, including U.S. Small Business Administration (SBA) "Small Business Journalist of the Year." His newsletter *The Business Owner Journal* has 35,000 paid subscribers and has earned many industry accolades.

Mr. Perkins is a talented and sought-after speaker. He is a member of the prestigious National Speakers Association, a Certified Toastmaster, and is available on a limited basis for keynote and breakout sessions for audiences of business owners.

Mr. Perkins earned a BA in psychology from the University of Oklahoma and an MBA from the University of Notre Dame. He resides in Tulsa, Oklahoma. Learn more at www.DLPerkins.com.

# SECTION 1

# Introduction

**What Is Business Valuation and Why Should I Understand It?** The everyday concepts of the business world are sales, management, marketing, accounting, inventory, purchasing, cash flow, borrowing, customers, vendors, insurance, etc. These concepts are what business owners, managers and professional advisors deal with daily. A much more evasive concept is business valuation. Business valuation is determining what a business is worth. It is the estimation of what a buyer would pay for a business. Knowledge of business valuation is not necessary to successfully start or manage a business, or to be a competent attorney, accountant, stockbroker or insurance agent. But having a basic understanding of value and business valuation will create a tremendous advantage.

**For the Business Owner.** If you own a business, your business is likely your largest investment. The quality of your retirement probably hinges on the proceeds that can be obtained from an eventual sale. To ensure your money, time and hard work yield returns, you should periodically check its value. To plan effectively, you should understand value and be able to constantly monitor it. Too many business owners accept myth and misconception about business valuation. They obtain rules of thumb from magazine articles, friends or advisors who mean well but have no real knowledge in the confusing area of business valuation. The result is disappointment and, at times, disaster.

**For the Future Business Owner.** You look for opportunity, but how will you assess it when it comes? Your skills at evaluating opportunity, and the action you take (or inaction) will have a more significant financial impact on you and your loved ones than all the other skills and abilities you possess, including education, experience, character, work ethic, vision, etc. Study this publication to build skills for assessing opportunity and value.

**For the Professional Advisor.** The success of any advisor depends on the knowledge and benefits he or she brings to the client. This holds true for all disciplines, but especially if you are an advisor to business owners such as an attorney, accountant or financial advisor. The goal of the business owner is to build wealth. A basic understanding of business valuation will provide a framework from which the advisor can put himself or herself in the shoes of the client and help him or her make decisions that build value – the ultimate service to any business owner.

**For the Employee Striving for Advancement.** Ask any business owner what he most wants from his employees. He or she will say, "I want them to think like me." Whether you are an entry-level employee, middle manager or top executive, knowledge of business valuation will set you apart from the pack and position you for advancement.

**For the Person Who Desires Wealth.** Look at anyone who has amassed significant wealth in a free society, and he or she will have been a great investor. The only way for anyone to build significant financial wealth is through investment. Wise investment, of course. A basic understanding of business valuation will provide the tools for successful investing – whether in a private business, public company or non-operating asset.

## Business valuation offers more to the business **OWNER** than the business seller.

---

*That's right. Business valuation is for the business* ***owner****. With an understanding of what drives business value, the business owner can take steps to build value. But doing so takes time. Wait until you want to sell your business and it'll be too late.*

**David L. Perkins, Jr.**

# Section 2

## Business Valuation: Confusing and Misunderstood

Do you want to know the value of your business? Pose the question to your closest friends and advisors. Write down your own answer and that of your spouse. You will be amazed at the range of responses. For further amusement, ask all of them how they arrived at their answers.

Although value and valuation are fundamental to our entire economic lives and free-market system, the concepts remain misunderstood and misapplied. Only a precious few possess a true working knowledge of valuation. From these few come the capitalists who earn 99 percent of the wealth today. They do so by combining their knowledge with capital and putting both to work. They are the ones on the front pages of our newspapers and financial journals.

Little wonder valuation is shrouded in confusion. Our high schools and colleges don't teach it (outside of basic microeconomic theory). Contrary to common belief, the basic curriculum for accountants and attorneys does not include business valuation. Most graduate business schools cover only the valuation of publicly traded securities. In addition, many would be surprised to find that bankers are not trained in business valuation and they almost never look at business value when assessing a loan. Note: For our purposes herein we use the terms income, profit and cash flow synonymously unless stated otherwise. Income is an accounting term. In a business, cash flow and income will be equal over time.

Unfortunately, business valuation has some inherent characteristics that foster confusion and misinformation, such as:

**Value is subjective:** Valuation is not exact but rather subjective. Like beauty, value is "in the eyes of the beholder." What is the value of the watch on your wrist? Or the diamond ring your spouse gave you? Or what about your father's prized possession – a 1971 Lincoln Continental parked, unprotected, in your backyard for the past eight years?

**Few People, Even Business People, Are Exposed to Factual Business Sale Data:** That so few of us own businesses means few experience the purchase or sale of a business firsthand. The biggie is that private business sale data are – well – private. As such, the data are scarcely available for public review and analysis. The result is: little factual information. This is in stark contrast to most regularly traded assets in our society, including stocks, bonds, real estate, automobiles, etc.

**High Interest and Few Factual Data Breed Misinformation:** For whatever reason, people in our culture are immensely interested in both people and money. Business sale transactions involve people and often a lot of money. Therefore, there is much interest in the terms of the sale. Combined with the fact that business sale data typically are not made available, misinformation quickly fills the void. This phenomenon is well documented in research studies. Add to this that the buyer or seller may allow or even seed false data, putting him or her in a favorable light.

**Complexity of Business Sale Transactions and Prevalence of "Terms":** Unlike cars and houses, businesses usually do not sell for 100 percent cash at closing. It is very common for part of the purchase price to be paid over time to the seller. If the time is long, then the nominal price (i.e., total dollars paid) and the real price (i.e., present value) may be quite different. It is also common for post-closing payments to be due, or forgiven, if certain events occur or fail to occur. As such, the actual sale price is often very difficult to determine.

**Each Business Is One of a Kind:** Most things we buy have identical or close substitutes. Even a used car or most houses can be considered to have very close substitutes. This makes the task of valuing much easier because we can compare it to others with similar characteristics. In contrast, businesses are almost all unique, rarely having close substitutes. Therefore, applying the "comparable sales" method is much more challenging. Finally, the coup de grace of confusion is that the question "What is the value?" has no definite answer unless the business is actually sold – and sold in a certain manner. Because the valuation task is often separate from an actual sale, value can only be estimated. In fact, this is precisely the valuation task. Nevertheless, to do so we must first answer four important questions:

- Value what?
- Value to whom?
- What definition of value?
- Value as of what date?

BUSINESS OWNERS IN THE U.S. WORK
52 HOURS PER WEEK, ON AVERAGE.

*(Selling a business takes between
200 and 600 hours of labor.)*

---

*And we can assume that the business owner works the long hours because the business needs it. If this is true, wouldn't we expect the business to suffer if the owner became distracted? In fact, this is exactly what happens when the business owner tries to handle the business sale himself or herself. Business performance suffers right in the thick of negotiations.*

**David L. Perkins, Jr.**

# SECTION 3

# Getting Started: Four Key Questions

Before any defensible attempt to estimate value can be made, four key questions must first be answered:

**Value What?** The first step is to clearly define what is being valued. If the subject is a going concern (an ongoing operating business), then what is being valued is typically the income stream the business generates. A business is nothing more than a group of assets – people, ideas, processes, products, equipment, etc. that produce an income stream for the owner or owners. Any assets not necessary for generation of the profit stream should be excluded from the appraisal and handled separately in a sale of the business. Any assets not actually owned by the business but necessary for generation of the profit stream need to be contributed to the business by the owner or the cost of acquiring the assets must be subtracted from the value conclusion. It also must be determined whether the appraisal is of the assets or equity of the business. An appraisal of the assets assumes the seller would retain all non-working liabilities (also referred to as "interest-bearing debt") of the business and, in a hypothetical sale, pay off these liabilities with funds received from the business sale. If the equity of the business is being valued, it is assumed the hypothetical buyer would get ALL assets of the business and assume ALL liabilities of the business as well. This equity (i.e., stock) versus assets question pertains to HOW the business is being purchased in addition to WHAT is being purchased, and impacts value in that it has significant implications for the tax costs to both buyer and seller.

**Value to Whom?** To estimate value, we must answer the question "Value to whom?" The answer can be an individual, investment group or another company. Once the question is answered, all the factors contributing to or detracting from the value of the subject, asset or business for the identified buyer must be considered. This type of value is referred to as *Investment Value.*

> *EXAMPLE: If we want to determine the value of XYZ Company to a Mr. Tenor, we would have to consider all the objective and subjective characteristics of XYZ Company as they relate to Mr. Tenor and his particular assets, interests, situation, capabilities, etc. Mr. Tenor may have a lifelong dream of owning XYZ Company and may have a particular aptitude that would allow him to grow the business significantly. Or Mr. Tenor may see ownership of XYZ Company as a burden he has no interest in bearing at any price.*
>
> *When our question is "What is the value of XYZ Company to Mr. Tenor?", then the value conclusion is influenced greatly by these factors. If the current owner/seller of XYZ Company (Mr. Seller) receives an offer from Mr. Tenor and responds, "I won't sell it for that," then the value of XYZ Company to Mr. Seller is greater than Mr.*

*Tenor's offer. Assuming Mr. Tenor offered 100 percent of what he is willing to pay, then a new buyer will have to be found if Mr. Seller hopes to sell the business at what he believes is the true value.*

**What Definition of Value?** The definition of value in the example above is investment value. The definition of investment value is described above as well. Another definition of value is *fair market value.* To explain, Mr. Seller in the above example could have a different value in mind altogether. Mr. Seller really wants to sell, and has not tried to ascertain the exact value XYZ Company has to him. He simply wants to sell the business for what it is worth. When we investigate further, he explains, "I want as much as I can get." Selling a business for maximum value can be a very frustrating task. First, what is the maximum value of a business? The reality is that nobody knows. How will Mr. Seller ever know if a particular offer he receives is the highest obtainable? Even if the price is the highest obtainable today, what about tomorrow? Business sellers enter into a very confusing and frustrating dilemma when the goal is value maximization. Add to this the possibility that the maximum value might include some seller financing. Mr. Seller must then consider, assuming the seller financing debt is not secured by assets outside of the business, whether the buyer will be able to run the business successfully and thereby generate cash flow sufficient to pay off the debt owed by the Buyer to the Seller. Faced with this dilemma, many sellers decide to go for fair market value, which is described in Section 4.

**Value As of What Date?** The fourth basic question to be answered before a business can be valued is "Value as of what date?" Of course, one could always assume the answer is today. But this is not always the case. In litigation, we often want to know what the value was on a particular date in the past. For instance the date of damage, breach, loss or death. Conversely, in finance we often need to predict what the value will be at some date in the future, such as when we expect a business or asset to be sold.

## Most business owners have a pretty good handle on what their business is worth.

*Wrong. Business owners often have a dollar amount in mind that they would sell for, but few know what price and terms are realistic. There's a big difference. First, unrealistically high expectations lead to wasted time and money, faulty plans and painful disappointments. Low expectations lead to a low price and less favorable terms. Second, you won't negotiate well if you don't understand where value comes from.*

**David L. Perkins, Jr.**

Section 4

# Basic Concepts of Business Valuation

**What Exactly Is *Value*?** *Value* is the utility, worth or desirability of an asset, right or privilege. In this publication, we will refer to all things of value as assets. In our society, assets are bought and sold with money. Therefore, value is expressed in dollars. The value of an asset to any single person or entity is simply the amount a person would pay to obtain it. A business is simply a group of assets. Business valuation is assigning a dollar value to a business by estimating what someone would pay to obtain the ownership rights. For the most part, an asset or group of assets has value only if it: (1) can be sold and turned into cash or (2) generates cash. The former is called *liquidation value* and the latter is called *going-concern value.* Both are discussed below.

**Going-Concern Value.** A business has value as a *going concern* only to the extent that it generates cash. If a business is to be operated as a going concern (i.e., it won't be liquidated), then its value is a function of the amount of cash or profits it will generate over time.

*Note: In this publication, cash, profits and income are used synonymously unless stated otherwise. Profit and income are the same thing and will, over time (in a no-growth business), equal cash flow.*

**Liquidation Value.** The amount of net cash obtained by selling the assets of a business piecemeal (not as a going concern) is *liquidation value.* "Net cash" means the sale proceeds less expenses incurred in the sale. For example, the value of a piece of real estate would be the price the asset could be sold for less any expenses of the sale, such as commission, legal and closing fees. Many assets don't generate income, such as an owner-occupied home. These assets, such as baseball cards, automobiles, furniture and equipment, don't have a going-concern value but only liquidation value. The value of such assets is limited to the cash generated from their liquidation.

**Liquidation Value vs. Going-Concern Value.** It can be said that every business has two potential values: *liquidation value* and *going-concern value.* We use the term "potential" because a business does not necessarily have value of both types.

For example, a business that consistently loses money may not have value as a going concern. Theoretically, such a business may have a negative going-concern value. But this is meaningless because the owner of such a business would quickly sell it to eliminate the economic erosion. The value received would be the liquidation value, or the sale price less sales expenses. Not to confuse the matter, but it is possible this business could sell as a going concern. To do so, a buyer would have to be found who believed he or she could operate the business profitably as a going concern. For the seller to obtain a price exceeding what could be obtained by liquidation, this buyer would have to be willing and able to pay more than the liquidation value. This would mean the buyer was willing and able to pay the seller for value the buyer brings to the business because of the buyer's skills, abilities, assets or competencies. Often, shrewd buyers will not do so unless they are worried a competing buyer might purchase the business or group of assets for a price greater than liquidation value.

The concepts of going-concern value and liquidation value also can lead to interesting predicaments. For example, consider a business with assets that could be liquidated (i.e., "sold off" individually) for $2 million but generates only $100,000 per year in profits. What is the value of this business? If the assets of the business are to be sold off, the value is clearly $2 million. If the business will not be liquidated, then the value is simply the income stream it generates.

So, what is the value of a $100,000 annual income stream? The answer depends on: (1) certainty with which the $100,000 will be received in the future ("risk"), and (2) value today of dollars received in the future ("time value of money"). Both of these concepts are discussed below.

**Time Value of Money.** Most people would rather receive a dollar today than in the future. As such, most people will pay less for a dollar received in the future compared to one received today. That a dollar received today can be deposited into a bank account to earn income supports the concept of time value of money. The mechanism used to adjust the value of a dollar received in the future into value today is called discounting. If one were to determine that he or she would pay just 80 cents for a dollar that was certain to be received in one year, then the discount rate is 25 percent. If the time value of money for this particular investor is consistent over time, then for every year a dollar's receipt will be delayed, a discount of 25 percent will be applied. The present value of a delayed payoff may be found by multiplying the payoff by a discount factor. If $C_1$ denotes the expected payoff at time period 1 (1 year from today), then:

$$\text{Present Value (PV)} = \text{Discount Factor} \times C_1$$

The discount factor is expressed as the reciprocal of 1 + rate of return:

$$\text{Discount Factor} = 1/(1+r)$$

*Where r = rate of return*

The rate of return (r) is the reward that investors demand for accepting delayed payment. If we use the numbers from the hypothetical example above, we find that $100,000 to be received in one year, discounted at 25 percent, is indeed $80,000.

$$\begin{aligned} PV &= [1/(1+.25)] \times \$100,000 \\ &= [1/1.25] \times \$100,000 \\ &= 0.80 \times \$100,000 \\ &= \$80,000 \end{aligned}$$

To illustrate how this concept is applied, let's assume that if we buy XYZ business, we will receive $100,000 at the end of each year for five years. To calculate the present value, we list the payment to be received in each year, then discount the dollars to the present value as follows:

| | Year 1 | Year 2 | Year 3 | Year 4 | Year 5 |
|---|---|---|---|---|---|
| Income to Be Received | $100,000 | $100,000 | $100,000 | $100,000 | $100,000 |
| Discount Rate* (@ 25% per year) | .800 | .640 | .512 | .409 | .328 |
| Present Value of Year's Cash Flow | $80,000 | $64,000 | $51,200 | $40,960 | $32,768 |
| Present Value of Business | | | | | $268,928 |

*Present value/discount rate conversion tables provided as an appendix herein.

The value of XYZ Company is $268,928 or the sum of the present values of each expected future cash payment. To avoid having to calculate each discount factor, refer to any present value table like the one at the back of this publication.

**Risk.** The degree of uncertainty of whether the expected returns will actually be realized is referred to as the risk of the investment. Because no investment is 100 percent certain to provide the expected return, investors discount the anticipated future cash flows by a rate greater than the standard for risk-free investment – U. S. Treasury obligations ("the risk-free rate"). When presented with an investment opportunity, one of the key tasks in assigning value is to estimate the risk. If we have no confidence that income will be received from the business (i.e., 0 percent), then we would pay nothing for the business (assuming the investment will have no liquidation value).

**Discount Rate.** *Time Value of Money*, discussed above, addresses how dollars received in the future are adjusted or discounted because the owner must wait for payment and forgo any and all potential benefits of having the money for use today. The rate at which future dollars are converted or discounted to present dollars is called the discount rate, also commonly referred to as the hurdle rate. The discount rate is made up of two components, the risk-free rate (to compensate for the time value of money) and the risk premium (to compensate for the riskiness of the investment – as in the uncertainty of the expected future cash flows). This can be represented by the equation:

$$R_f + R = D$$

*Where $R_f$ is the risk-free rate*
*R is the risk premium and*
*D is the discount rate*

**Risk-Free Rate.** If the receipt of expected future cash flow was guaranteed, then the discount rate used to translate future receipts into present dollars would be the risk-free rate. The financial world looks to U.S. government bills as the benchmark for risk-free investments. In other words, the financial world believes with 100 percent certainty the United States Government will pay its debts in full, and on time. As such, we can look at the rate of return or yield paid or earned on U.S. obligations as a representation of the time value of money for investors.

In theory, to entice investors to contribute money to an investment that is risk-free, a rate of return equal to at least that paid on U.S. obligations would be required. A one-year U.S. Treasury bill today earns around 3 percent per year. If we determined there was uncertainty as to whether a proposed investment would actually pay the expected returns, then in theory the investor would require a higher return to compensate for such risk. If we take our same investment example from above, which is expected to return $100,000 at the end of each year for five consecutive years and apply the risk-free rate, the value of this hypothetical business would be $458,691 calculated as follows:

| | Year 1 | Year 2 | Year 3 | Year 4 | Year 5 |
|---|---|---|---|---|---|
| Income to Be Received | $100,000 | $100,000 | $100,000 | $100,000 | $100,000 |
| Discount Rate* (@ 3% per year) | .971 | .943 | .915 | .888 | .862 |
| Present Value of Year's Cash Flow | $97,087 | $94,260 | $91,514 | $88,849 | $86,261 |
| Present Value of Business | | | | | $458,691 |

*Present value/discount rate conversion tables provided as an appendix herein.

**Return on Investment.** Generally referred to as the cash or profit gained from equity dollars invested. This is also referred to as *Return on Equity* (ROE). The return can be expressed as a dollar amount, or converted to a percentage by dividing the return by the equity deployed. Typically, returns are calculated on an annual basis and referred to as annual *rate of return.*

$$\frac{\text{Dollars Received}}{\text{Dollars Originally Invested}} = \text{Rate of Return}$$

Return also can be calculated on total capitalization (debt and equity). Such a return would be calculated as follows:

$$\frac{\text{Dollars Received}}{\text{(Equity Capital + Debt Capital Invested)}} = \text{RTC}$$

*Where RTC = Return on Total Capitalization*

*EXAMPLE: If $50 were received in year 1 as a return on $200 invested, the rate of return would be 25 percent.*

When considering the discount rate or required return on investment, it is helpful to study the historical returns of various investments. The table below lists the average annual total returns earned on a variety of investments during the modern era in the United States. Each of the investments in the list is publicly traded. If we consider the character of the investments listed and the returns of each, we can make some general conclusions as the required rates of return on investments that are not listed below, such as private (non-public) investments.

| **Table 4.1** | **Average Annual Returns**[2] |
|---|---|
| Inflation | 3.1% |
| U.S. Treasury Bills (30 days) | 3.8% |
| U.S. Treasury Bonds (5 years) | 5.5% |
| U.S. Treasury Bonds (20 years) | 5.8% |
| L.T. Corporate Bonds (20 years) | 6.0% |
| Large-Cap Stocks | 12.4% |
| Micro-Cap Stocks[1] | 19.0% |

Source: SBBI Valuation Edition 2005 Yearbook. Returns are the average annual total (income and capital appreciation) arithmetic mean for 1926 to 2004 in the United States.

[1] Micro-Cap Stocks is defined as the portfolio of stocks comprising the 9th and 10th deciles of the New York Stock Exchange. According to the Center for Research in Security Prices, University of Chicago, the average capitalization of micro-cap companies from 1926 to 2004 was $175 million.

[2] Returns are return to total capitalization (debt and equity).

Each investment listed in the table above is publicly traded, thus marketable, and can be sold quickly, easily and inexpensively. The lowest-risk investments generally are considered to be U.S. government obligations. As we can see in the table, these obligations pay – as we would expect – a lower rate of return. The lowest is the 30-day Treasury note. If you give up the rights to your money for just 30 days, then you have less risk than with, say, the 5-year note, but you get paid a lower return. What risk is there, given that these are U.S. government obligations? Mainly, risk associated with the uncertainly of the degree to which inflation will erode the real value of your money (during the time you give up the rights to it). The highest was from micro-cap stocks at 19 percent annually.

**Rates of Return for Public Equities.** Let's also look at the table titled "Rates of Return by Size of Public Company." It shows the historical average annual rate of return for various sizes of publicly traded companies. Size is determined by total market capitalization, which is simply the value of the company as set by the public (i.e., the shares are publicly traded).

**Rates of Return by Size of Public Company**

| Average Company Value | Annual Return* |
|---|---|
| $880 million | 15.7% |
| $591 million | 16.7% |
| $391 million | 17.7% |
| $104 million | 21.8% |

Source: Ibbotson Associates

* Arithmetic Mean

What you see is – SIZE MATTERS. The largest public companies have earned, on average over the past 75 years, 11.4 percent. The smallest — 21.8 percent (nearly double!).

But what is a fair annual rate of return for a private company? Good question. Private-company rate of return data are not widely available. The reason? Because private companies are, well, private. That is, the data are not recorded anywhere and available for public review. But we can make inferences from the information that IS available. Namely, the rates of return earned and accepted on public investments, such as those in the accompanying tables.

First, if we look at Table 4.1, we see that as the size of the company declines, rates of return rise. The smallest public companies – averaging $104 million value – have returned 21.8 percent annually, on average, over the past 75 years.

Section 14 describes some very important differences between public and private companies. In sum, small private companies are much riskier than their public peers and thus command a higher return for their owners. Their owners DESERVE a higher rate of return – to compensate them for the risk that they bear.

Finally, as the market capitalization (i.e., "size" or equity value) declines, the rate of return curves northward. One could attempt to project the line out and thereby estimate what it might be for companies that are smaller still. Clearly, the rate of return would cross over 25 percent very quickly. The primary reasons are as follows:

- The average private company will be less marketable than the average publicly traded micro-cap-size company, thus will have more risk.
- The average private company will be smaller than the average publicly traded micro-cap-size company, thus will have poorer access to equity and debt capital, and higher capital costs.

**Control.** *Control* is the ability of an owner or shareholder of a business to influence how the business is operated. Generally, control is associated with an ownership percentage that exceeds 50 percent, so votes that require majority can be won by the "controlling" shareholder. Non-controlling owners are referred to as minority interests. Controlling interests typically will sell for higher values than non-controlling positions, leading to what is referred to as control premiums and minority discounts. Studies have documented lack-of-control discounts averaging 25 percent to 30 percent for publicly traded companies. Similarly, premiums offered for controlling positions are going from the 35 percent to 45 percent ranges.

**Marketability.** The certainty to which an investment can be liquidated and turned into cash within a reasonable period is called marketability. Actively traded public securities such as shares of a public company traded on a major stock exchange are considered highly marketable. Such shares can be turned into cash within a few days. Real property (i.e., real estate) has typically poor marketability, depending on the location and overall desirability. Controlling interests in private companies are marketable but, like real estate, can take six months or more to be turned into cash, not to mention the time and expense necessary to do so. Assets that have good marketability typically sell for higher values than those with poor marketability. Minority positions in private companies are considered highly unmarketable because the lack-of-control characteristic is considered highly undesirable. Extensive studies have been conducted on this topic. The evidence shows that private companies will tend to trade at prices 35 percent to 50 percent below their publicly traded counterparts.

**Fair Market Value.** Fair market value is the most commonly used method for valuing businesses, real estate or other kind of assets. The definition sidesteps the "value to whom" question and replaces it with the following:

> *The price at which an asset would change hands between a willing buyer and willing seller, both of whom are reasonably knowledgeable of the pertinent facts and neither of whom is under any compulsion to act.*

The definition of *fair market value* ignores the characteristics a particular buyer may have that might lead to compulsions or synergies (i.e., investment value).

**Investment Value, Financial Value and Synergistic Value.** If a particular buyer of an asset or business is identified, our task becomes to estimate the value the asset or business has to this particular buyer. Our definition then is not *fair market value* but *investment value.* Individuals or entities will each value goods, services and assets differently. For example, a fisherman who lives on the ocean might find significant value in a new fishing boat, while a Nevada miner who gets seasick might have very little interest in the same boat. The answer to the question "value to whom" discussed above is critical. If the particular buyer identified has characteristics or capabilities that may enable it to earn returns that go beyond what the seller-company is capable of producing on a stand-alone basis, then the buyer is referred to as a *synergistic buyer. Synergistic buyers* have businesses, assets or capabilities that, when combined with the selling company's business, assets or capabilities, will yield benefits (income) unique to the particular business combination. The subject business will yield higher returns, when acquired, than it would by remaining independent.

Buyers looking solely to the subject investment or business to yield returns and have no synergistic characteristics, assets or capabilities that will add to the return on investment of a particular business are referred to as *financial buyers.* Individuals are typically *financial buyers.*

**Tangible and Intangible Assets.** A business is simply a compilation of assets, both tangible and intangible. *Tangible assets* are things that can be touched, things the average person tends to be more familiar with. Tangible assets are more commonly bought and sold, and include cash, inventory, equipment and real estate. Because they are more commonly bought and sold, tangible assets are typically easier to value and sell.

*Intangible assets* are things that cannot be physically seen or touched and are not commonly bought and sold. For this reason they are more difficult to value, less understood and harder to turn into cash. Intangible assets include trade names, reputation, customer lists, relationships, patents, trademarks, location, management talent and proprietary databases, processes, products and recipes.

**Goodwill and Blue Sky.** *Goodwill* is defined as the intangible asset that may arise or exist in a business enterprise as a result of the name, reputation, competency, location, product, service, customer lists, etc. Such value, when it exists, is separate and distinct from the tangible assets of a business enterprise. Goodwill is also the term accountants use for the portion of a purchase price paid for a business in excess of the book value of the business' assets. *Blue sky* is slang for goodwill. Generally speaking, people or organizations buy businesses to earn a profit. If this is true, then buyers will be willing to buy businesses only if they believe a profit can be earned over and above the cost of the purchase. If the profit expectation compels a buyer to pay a price exceeding the book value of the assets of the business, then goodwill or blue sky will have been paid. Contrary to common belief, a business does not have goodwill simply because it has been in business, unless such attributes contribute to its future profitability – or perceived value.

## Marketing that appeals to reason has no appeal at all.

*Aristotle agrees. It's not enough to appeal to reason and logic. You must appeal to emotion. Marketing a business is about packaging and persuasion. You must connect before you convince. Emotion is the vehicle. Facts are the passengers.*

**David L. Perkins, Jr.**

# SECTION 5

# Three Basic Approaches to Valuation

**Market Approach.** This is a general way of determining the value of a business or any asset by using one or more methods comparing the subject company to similar businesses. It is commonly used to value real estate and is often referred to as the comparable sales method. To apply this method to the valuation of a private company, a comparable sale must be found. This can be a difficult task. And the conclusion will be useful only if the data are reliable, the comparisons parallel, and the guideline company (or companies) are similar to the company being valued. Parallel means, for example, if the guideline company data use net profit after tax, then the indicated multiple should use the same type of profit from the company being valued (net profit after tax).

To apply this method, follow these steps:

1. Locate Comparable Sale Data. For each comparable transaction, you must have, at a minimum, annual revenue,

annual profit, the total price paid and the terms of sale (i.e., percentage down, percentage financed by the seller, percentage contingency or earn-out, what assets were included in the purchase and what debt the buyer assumed). The exact definition of profit must be obtained to be sure the comparison is parallel. Asset values and trends in revenues and earnings would be helpful to draw comparisons to the subject company.

Comparable sales data for private companies can be difficult and costly to locate. Three groups maintain comparable sale databases on small and midsize private companies – Pratt Stats, BIZCOMPS and the Institute of Business Appraisers. An Internet search under each will quickly allow you to locate the data. If publicly traded companies are used to estimate the value of a private company, one must find comparables with characteristics in common with the subject company, such as size, profit margins, growth rate, products and industries served. Even if this is possible, adjustments for both control and marketability incompatibilities must be made.

2. Calculate the key ratios for each sale, such as price-to-revenue, price-to-earnings, and price-to-tangible assets. For example, let us assume we found a guideline company that sold for $1,000,000 – 50 percent cash at closing and 50 percent seller financing. Revenues were $3,000,000 and annual profits were $333,333 per year. We can calculate the following:

- Price to Revenue was 0.333 ($1,000,000/$3,000,000)
- Price to Earnings was 3.0 ($1,000,000/$333,333)

When we do so for each guideline company, we can prepare a table with the following results:

| | Price to Revenue | Price to Earnings | Price to Tangible Assets |
|---|---|---|---|
| Guideline Company A | 0.7 | 5.0 | 2.0 |
| Guideline Company B | 0.9 | 10.0 | 3.0 |
| Guideline Company C | 1.1 | 15.0 | 5.0 |
| Average | 0.9 | 10.0 | 3.33 |

3. Compare these numbers to the revenue, earnings and tangible assets of the company being valued. The result will be indications of value. For example:

| | Subject Company | Average Multiplier | Value Indication |
|---|---|---|---|
| Subject Co. Annual Rev. | $5,000,000 | .9 | $4,500,000 |
| Subject Co. Annual Earnings | $500,000 | 10.0 | $5,000,000 |
| Subject Co. Tangible Assets | $1,000,000 | 3.33 | $3,333,333 |
| **Average of Value Indications** | | | **$4,277,778** |

The value conclusion could be a subjective opinion as to which indicator has the most relevance, or which guideline company has such. Or the conclusion could be the average of the indications.

4. Adjust the conclusion, if needed. For example, if you are valuing a minority stake in a private company, but your comparables are all sales of controlling interests of private companies, you need to apply a lack-of-control discount to the value conclusion. To illustrate:

| | |
|---|---|
| Value Indication – 100 percent: | $4,277,778 |
| Percent being valued: | x .40 |
| Subtotal | $1,711,111 |
| Less lack-of-control discount (33 percent): | ($564,667) |
| Estimated Value of 40 percent Position: | $1,146,445 |

*Where to find the data:* Data on publicly traded companies are widely available today. Online sources include www.edgar-online.com and www.yahoo.com. Search by SIC code or industry description. Data on private companies can be obtained from Mergerstat, Pratt Stats, Institute of Business Appraisers and BIZCOMPS.

*Note: When valuing a company by comparing it to other companies or groups of companies, it is imperative that the data for the sample set are collected in the same way as the data on the subject company, and vice versa. For example, one must ensure the level of earnings used for the company being valued is the same as the sample set. In this case, the earnings reported by public companies are after-tax income (i.e., net income) prepared on an accrual basis using generally accepted accounting principles (GAAP). The after-tax net income of the subject company should be used. If the income statements of the subject company are not prepared on an accrual basis according to GAAP, then an adjustment must be made for the results to be reliable.*

*Reconciling Business Debt and the Value Conclusion:* The business seller is interested in the net proceeds to him or her. But care must always be taken to know what is being valued and how to translate it into a "net to seller" conclusion. In other words, one must be sure to compare "apples to apples," with respect to how debt is treated and what is being valued. In most cases, when the market method is used, the comparable examples will have valued the following:

- All assets are necessary to support the ongoing operations of the business, including a normal level of cash, receivables, accruals and inventory
- A normal level of trade debt
- Exclude all long-term and interest-bearing liabilities of the business

If one uses comparables as described above and this definition is used, then the long-term and interest-bearing debt of the subject company must be subtracted from the value conclusion to produce the estimate of pretax net to owner. Regardless, the appraiser must pay attention to how the comparables were valued and how to calculate a "net-to-owner" conclusion.

**Income Approach.** This is a general way of determining the value of a business, or any assets, by using one or more methods that convert anticipated benefits into a present, single amount.

*Discounted Future Cash Flows Method* – This method simply involves estimating the future income of the business, then discounting the dollars to the present. When estimating income, any interest expense should be added back before any calculations are performed. The discount rate used is a function of the time value of money and the risk in the business. See *time value of money, discount rate* and *risk* discussed in the section titled "Basic Concepts of Business Valuation." The methodology is identical to that described under the *time value of money* section.

*Capitalized Future Economic Income Method* – This method produces a value conclusion by calculating the present value of future income, just as the DFCF methods does above, but is easier to apply. But it can be used only when the projected income or cash flow meets one of these two conditions:

(1) Projected income is identical in each projected year.

(2) Projected income grows at a constant rate in each projected year.

If condition 1 is met, the following formula can be applied to produce the value conclusion:

$$PV = E/k$$

*Where PV = Present Value*

*E = Expected Income in Each Future Year (or Period)*

*k = Discount Rate*

For example, ABC Company projects a pretax annual income of $100,000 each year. We can convert this income stream into a value by dividing $100,000 by a discount rate appropriate for the risk characteristics of this business and the desired return of the investor. If the rate is 25 percent, calculate the value as follows:

$$PV = \$100{,}000/.25 = \$400{,}000$$

If condition 2 is met, the following formula can be applied to produce the value conclusion:

$$PV = E1/(k - g)$$

*Where PV = Present Value*

*E1 = Expected Income in Year One*

*k = Discount Rate*

*g = Annual Growth Rate of Expected Income*

*And k - g = Capitalization Rate*

For example, XYZ Company projects $100,000 of pretax income in year 1 and expects the income to grow each year by 10 percent. The value of XYZ can be estimated as follows:

$$
\begin{aligned}
PV &= \$100{,}000/(.25 - .10) \\
&= \$100{,}000/.15 \\
&= \$666{,}667
\end{aligned}
$$

*Note: When estimating income, any interest expense should be added back before any calculations are performed.*

*Reconciling Business Debt and the Value Conclusion:* The business seller is interested in the sale proceeds he or she gets to keep. But the value conclusion in the income approach, as we have described it, includes only a normal level of working capital debt such as trade payables and company accruals. To determine the equity value of the business, subtract from the value conclusion all company debt exceeding a normal level of working capital debt. What is normal can be determined from data of industry peers obtained from trade associations or RMA Statements Studies (search the Internet under the same name). For example, if XYZ Company had non-working debt of $400,000, then the equity value of the business would be $267,667 ($666,667 - $400,000). This is the net amount the business seller receives from the sale before taxes.

**Asset Approach.** This is a general way of determining the value of a business, or any assets, by quantifying the amount of money required to replace the future service capability of that asset. There are two primary asset approach methods: asset accumulation method and liquidation method.

*Asset Accumulation Method (AAM)*: When applying the asset accumulation method, we answer the following question: "What would it cost to create or construct, at current prices, the company with equivalent utility?" The methodology used is represented by the following equation:

Value = RCN – Functional Obsolescence

*Where RCN = Replacement Cost New*

Calculating the replacement cost new (RCN) requires identification of all costs incurred in the re-creation of the assets of the business that are functionally identical to those being valued. All costs will fall into one of the following four categories:

- Material – Expenditures related to the tangible elements of the intangible asset development process.
- Labor – Expenditures related to the human capital efforts necessary to develop the intangible asset.
- Overhead – Expenditures necessary to oversee the project, including: management, supervision, support and clerical labor, necessary payroll taxes, perquisites and benefits, utilities and operating expenses.
- Developer's Profit – The profit required by whoever is charged with creating or developing the intangible asset.

If the assets being valued are not new, then it is possible the newly created asset is of greater utility than the one being duplicated (the "old" one). If this is the case, the ones being valued may have functional obsolescence, which is defined as the reduction in value due to its inability to perform the function for which it was originally designed. An adjustment must be made to the RCN value as the formula offered above represents.

*Liquidation Method*: When we apply the liquidation method we simply answer the question *"What cash would be generated, net of liabilities and liquidation costs, if the assets of the business were sold?"* Often this entails selling the assets off piece by piece. The approach here is self-explanatory, so we will not go into a detailed explanation. Auction houses or brokers could be enlisted to assist in the sale of the assets.

*Reconciling Business Debt and the Value Conclusion*: The business seller is interested in the sale proceeds he or she gets to keep. When the liquidation method is applied, it is easy to see that the seller will get to keep the cash left over after he or she has sold all the assets and paid off the debt. But if an asset approach is used to determine a value for the going concern, such as in the asset accumulation method (AAM), the seller must not forget that the value conclusion assumes no debt. For example, if the AAM method was used and determined it would cost $1,000,000 to assemble a company with capabilities similar to the subject company, then the assets of the subject company would be worth $1,000,000. If the subject company had $500,000 in debt, then the equity value of the company would be $500,000. The buyer would be willing to pay, either by providing value (cash) or assuming obligations of the seller (debts of the company), no more than the $1,000,000. The seller could either sell the entire company for $500,000 and have the buyer assume the debt, bringing the total paid for the business to $1,000,000 or the seller could sell the assets of the business, free of debt, to the buyer for $1,000,000 and pay off the liabilities – again netting $500,000 pretax.

## A BUSINESS WITH A LONG HISTORY WILL BE WORTH MORE THAN A NEW BUSINESS.

---

*This is a common misconception. In the real world, if an asset does not contribute to higher profit, it has no value. In other words, a long history is meaningless unless it contributes to the bottom line. History won't pay the bills.*

**David L. Perkins, Jr.**

# SECTION 6

# Recasting Financial Statements

**How and Why to Adjust Financial Statements.** Buyers of private companies purchase businesses for the profit they generate, or can generate. They look at the past as an indicator of the business' ability to generate cash, or profits. They also look at the value of the assets, liabilities and equity of the business. For private companies, the financial statements often do not reflect the true profitability and asset values of the business. This is because:

- Accrual accounting can distort the reported profits and balance sheet values of assets and liabilities.
- There are many ways a business owner can eliminate value, or earnings, to reduce the bottom line.
- Tax reduction strategies are used to reduce the reported profit.
- Value of assets and liabilities on the balance sheet can change over time, and may not be reflected on the balance sheet.

Therefore, to obtain an accurate estimate of value, one must adjust the income statements and balance sheets to show the true profitability of the business and the true value of the assets and liabilities.

**Income Statement Adjustments.** Common income statement adjustments include the following:

- *Excessive owner compensation:* compensation exceeding what it would cost to hire someone to perform the duties of the owner or owners.
- *Expenses not necessary for the ongoing operation of the business:* may include expensive cars or trucks, excessive travel, etc.
- *Non-recurring expenses:* one-time bad debt write-offs, non-recurring operating losses, legal fees, etc.
- *Non-cash expenses:* Amortization should be eliminated altogether. Depreciation expense should be removed and replaced with the actual amount that needs to be invested annually into the fixed asset base of the business – to maintain the production capacity of these assets.

*Example: XYZ Company Historical Financial Statements with Adjustments (below).*

Although future income is what business buyers consider when assigning value, historical performance provides the basis for the projection. This is the reason historical income statements should be adjusted.

### XYZ Company Historical Income Statements

| | 2002 | 2003 | 2004 | 2005 |
|---|---|---|---|---|
| Revenue | $1,000 | $1,200 | $1,150 | $1,400 |
| Cost of Goods | (600) | (720) | (700) | (840) |
| Gross Profit | 400 | 480 | 450 | 560 |
| Operating Expense | (364) | (409) | (371) | (467) |
| Operating Profit | 36 | 71 | 71 | 93 |
| Taxes and Other | (11) | (21) | (21) | (28) |
| Net Income | 25 | 50 | 50 | 65 |
| *Adjustments* | | | | |
| Excess Owner Compensation | $100 | $110 | $110 | $125 |
| Depreciation | $50 | $50 | $50 | $50 |
| Non-Recurring Legal Fees | $0 | $50 | $0 | $0 |
| Owner Benefits in Excess of Market | $50 | $50 | $70 | $70 |
| Taxes | $11 | $21 | $21 | $28 |
| Total Adjustments | $211 | $251 | $251 | $273 |
| **Adjusted Pretax Net Income** | **$236** | **$331** | **$301** | **$338** |

**Balance Sheet Adjustments.** Common balance sheet adjustments include:

- *Accounts receivable*: to reflect the actual collectable amount.
- *Inventory*: to reflect the value of the inventory that is actually sellable, at cost.
- *Cash*: exclude cash that will not be sold with the business.

- Other assets: any asset that will not be sold with the business, or would not have real value to a new owner, should be excluded.
- Fixed assets and real property should be listed at their current fair market values.
- Depreciation should be eliminated altogether and replaced with the actual amount that needs to be invested into the fixed asset base of the business – to maintain the production capacity of these assets.
- Debt should reflect the actual payoff value of the obligations of the company, or at least those that a prospective new buyer would assume.

The standard of value that should be used for the adjusted balance sheet is fair market value (for a definition, see Section 4). Because fair market value can be truly determined only in an actual sale, these values are estimated. And although there will be no liquidation of assets in a sale of a business as a going concern, the true market value of such assets is important to both the buyer and seller. This is because the lowest price a buyer should accept is the sum of the values of the underlying assets themselves. Restating the assets and liabilities of the business provides an accurate picture for the buyer and seller, which eliminate uncertainty. In addition, it will help the buyer estimate the amount he or she can borrow against the assets to apply toward the purchase. The higher the amount that can be borrowed, the higher the purchase price that can be paid.

## XYZ Balance Sheet – Adjusted

| | YE 2005 Actual | YE 2005 Adjusted | Difference |
|---|---|---|---|
| Cash | $100 | $0 | ($100) |
| Receivables | $400 | $375 | ($25) |
| Inventory | $400 | $350 | ($50) |
| Other Current Assets | $50 | $0 | ($50) |
| *Total Current Assets* | *$950* | *$725* | |
| Furniture, Fixtures and Equipment Net of Depreciation | $200 | $400 | $200 |
| Real Estate | $250 | $400 | $150 |
| Other Fixed Assets | $40 | $0 | ($40) |
| *Total Long-Term Assets* | *$490* | *$800* | |
| **Total Assets** | **$1,440** | **$1,525** | **$85** |
| | | | |
| Trade Payables | $300 | $300 | $0 |
| Other Current Liabilities | $100 | $100 | $0 |
| *Total Current Liabilities* | *$400* | *$400* | |
| Long-Term Debt | $650 | $650 | $0 |
| Note Payable To Owner | $50 | $0 | ($50) |
| *Total Long-Term Debt* | *$700* | *$800* | |
| **Total Liabilities** | **$1,100** | **$1,050** | **($50)** |
| | | | |
| Equity | $340 | $475 | $135 |
| **Total Debt And Equity** | **$1,440** | **$1,525** | **$85** |

## "I'M VERY CONCERNED ABOUT CONFIDENTIALITY, SO I WANT TO JUST HANDLE THE SALE MYSELF."

*Yes, confidentiality is critical. But are you going to maintain it by handling the sale yourself? So, when you talk to buyers you'll, ah, wear a disguise?*

*P.S. A qualified representative can mask the identity of a client until late in the process.*

**David L. Perkins, Jr.**

# SECTION 7

## How to Handle the Balance Sheet

The price paid for a business is established by estimating the future profit or cash flow and then applying an appropriate or fair rate of return based on the riskiness of the investment. When the price of a going concern is established, the price is usually justified by the profits the business will generate. Typically, it is assumed that the business will begin paying the appropriate amount of profit (or cash flow) on the first day the new owner takes control. But if the seller pushes deal terms that do not allow for this, then the logical and knowledgeable buyer would required a price adjustment to make up for the impact to profit or cash flow.

For example, if the seller wants to retain accounts receivable (i.e., not include them as part of the assets purchased by the buyer), then the buyer would have to wait 30 days to begin receiving any cash (assuming company sales are made on net 30 terms) and the buyer would never regain the cash he or she did not receive during the first 30 days. If the lost cash amounted to $25,000, the buyer should be willing to pay $25,000 less than he or she would with the accounts receivable included in the purchased assets.

Similarly, if a buyer received the accounts receivable with the purchase, but the seller paid off the accounts payable himself or herself, then the buyer would begin receiving cash from sales on day 1 but would not have to pay any bills for 30 days, assuming most purchases are made on net 30 terms. In theory, this buyer should be willing to pay more for this business because cash flow during the first 30 days will exceed the level used in valuing the business.

For this reason, most businesses are sold with the buyer acquiring all receivables and accrued assets and assuming the accounts payable and accrued liabilities. These accounts are referred to as working accounts. The net of the two is referred to as working capital. Another way to accomplish the same cash-neutral effect is for the seller to keep all working assets and all working liabilities.

Non-working debts of the company – such as borrowings and notes – are debts that must be repaid, even in a going concern. Such debts may be retained and paid by the seller or assumed by the buyer. But a buyer should not be willing to pay the full price for the business PLUS assume non-working debts. For example, if a business is valued at $500,000 and the buyer gets all assets of the business and assumes all working debt, the buyer should not be willing to ALSO assume any non-working debt. If the seller wishes for the buyer to assume, say $200,000 in non-working debt, then the buyer should do so only if the price is reduced by an equal amount, to $300,000 in our example.

## If you have just one buyer, who has whom?

---

***co·nun·drum*** *\ n.\ something confusing, puzzling or mysterious.*

*Deal with one buyer at a time and you have no leverage. Multiple buyers provide you with bargaining power.*

**David L. Perkins, Jr.**

# Section 8

## What Do Small and Midsize Businesses Really Sell For?

Some 95 percent of businesses in the United States post annual gross revenues of less than $2 million per year. Despite this, hard data about the price these businesses sell for are not well documented or disseminated. The primary reason is that sale data were not extensively gathered and analyzed. But in recent years the available resources have improved somewhat because three groups now track small-business sale data – Institute of Business Appraisers, Pratt's Stats and BIZCOMPS.

To provide you with a general understanding of what small and midsize businesses sell for, let's revisit some of the information we covered in Section 4, namely the "Rates of Return by Size of Public Company" table, reproduced on the following page. The investments in the table are all publicly traded. As such, data on them are widely available to the public. In contrast, data are not widely available on private investment rates of return.

**Rates of Return by Size of Public Company**

| Average Company Value | Annual Return* |
|---|---|
| $880 million | 15.7% |
| $591 million | 16.7% |
| $391 million | 17.7% |
| $104 million | 21.8% |

Source: Ibbotson Associates

* Arithmetic Mean

We can see that micro-cap stocks – publicly traded companies with an average market value of their equity of $175 million – have returned, on average, 19 percent pretax over the years 1926 to 2004. Public companies with average values of $104 million have average annual returns of 21.8 percent. All these companies (discussed further in Section 14) have characteristics that provide the investor with a much lower level of risk compared to the typical small or midsize private company. These characteristics include the fact that owners of public company shares may liquidate their investment in about five days—an immensely valuable characteristic—compared to the very liquid nature of private company investments. For this reason and for those listed in Section 14, buyers of public companies will typically require rates of return far in excess of the return they could receive from investment in micro-cap stocks. Consider as well that the prospective buyer of a small or midsize private company has the choice of applying his capital toward the purchase of the private company, and then actively managing it to ensure he receives his return. Or he or she could put the money in a publicly traded small-cap stock fund and, while lying on the beach, enjoy an 18.4 percent return on average—assuming the future will reflect the past.

Most small and midsize private companies sell for between two and four times the normalized annual income (pretax and pre-interest). Volumes of data support this. The brevity of this publication will not allow for presentation of extensive amounts of these data, but surveys conducted by the International Business Brokers Association, for example, support this range.

A valuation multiple of three times the pretax income of a business represents a 33 percent return on total capital invested. To illustrate, assume a company earns $100,000 per year pretax. A three-times multiple would mean the company sells for $300,000. The return on investment (total capitalization) would be 33 percent or $100,000 divided by $300,000. Similarly, a multiple of four equals a 25 percent return on investment. For a small, private company to command a five-times multiple, it would have to be very special indeed, considering the returns offered by other less risky investments as described above and in Section 4.

Shedding light on what very small companies sell for, for example, is a publication titled *Transaction Patterns* by Toby Tatum. The report shares the results of his extensive analysis of the roughly 4,000 business sale transactions documented in the BIZCOMPS database. The results may be chilling to many business owners yet could explain the frustration many endure when trying to sell. Below is a reproduction of some of the key results.

- Businesses sell for 49 percent of annual revenue, on average.
- Businesses sell for 2.4 times seller's discretionary cash flow (SDCF), on average.

- 70 percent of all small businesses sold include seller financing.
- Of transactions that include seller financing, the most frequent percentage of total price financed by the seller is 50 percent.
- Of transactions that include seller financing, 70 percent of notes are amortized over five years or less.
- The payback period for the buyer's down payment has a mean of 1.1 years and an average of 1.5 years.

The average selling price in the BIZCOMPS database was $271,000 and the mean selling price was $127,000. Small companies indeed! Also, the selling price is calculated by totaling the consideration paid for the inventory; furniture, fixtures and equipment; and intangible assets of the business. Excluded from the purchase price is consideration paid for accounts receivable, if any. Consideration includes cash paid and liabilities assumed, whether trade debt, seller financing or other.

The earnings value used in this study is Sellers Discretionary Cash Flow (SDCF), defined as annual pretax profit plus the total annual compensation and benefits paid to a single owner. To this total are added non-cash expenses such as depreciation, amortization and any interest paid on long-term debt. Also added are any non-recurring expenses and/or expenses not necessary for the ongoing operation of the business. Likewise, any additional expenses a new owner would incur in running the business have been subtracted.

Although these data can help the business owner estimate the market value for his or her business, business valuation is a complex discipline. Before relying on any results, the business seller should consult an experienced appraiser or business broker.

## Nobody cares about your business.

*That's right. Business buyers just want to make a lot of money. So quit trying to find a buyer who shares your love for your business and people. Sell what they're buying.*

**David L. Perkins, Jr.**

# Section 9

# Making Sense of the Sales Multiple

We all have heard that companies sell on "multiples of earnings." As such, the talk at the club or trade conference has quickly moved to who sold for the highest multiple. We hear the multiples, but we almost never hear the definition of profit used or important elements such as the deal terms.

The truth is, there is much confusion about profits and earnings. A recent *Wall Street Journal* article recognized this, stating that there are a "host of names for...earnings and there is no uniform standard by which to understand them, causing much confusion among investors." Because of this, the definition used should always be clarified.

This section will explain the various types of "profits" used, and the definitions of each. With an understanding of the terms and definitions, we can put any particular business sale multiple into proper perspective.

To begin, review the 2001 income statement for XYZ Company on page 60. How much profit did XYZ make in 2001? This is a trick question.

Profit comes in many forms. Gross Profit. Operating Profit. Net Profit. Taxable Profit. Earnings can be taken to mean the same as profits. The names and definitions are almost endless. Below is a list of commonly used terms that refer to the profitability of a business.

**Gross Profit** – Revenue minus direct costs
(Direct expenses are often referred to as cost of goods sold.)

**Operating Profit** – Gross Profit minus Operating Expenses (Operating expenses are often referred to as sales, general and administrative expenses.)

**Pretax Profit** – Operating Profit minus any non-operating expenses (except taxes). Non-operating expenses are unusual expenses such as gains/losses on the sale of assets; non-recurring expenses; gains and losses on the sale of investments; costs associated with events that will never occur again, etc.

**After-Tax Profit** – Profit after <u>all</u> expenses have been deducted, including taxes.

**Net Profit** – *See "After-Tax Profit."*

**Profit** – A general term for profitability. Examples include gross profit and net profit.

**Earnings** – A term for profit. Generally considered to mean net profit or after-tax profit.

**EBIT** – Earnings Before Interest and Taxes.

**EBITDA** – Earnings Before Interest, Taxes, Depreciation and Amortization.

**Seller's Discretionary Cash Flow (SDCF)** – EBITDA plus owner compensation plus all expenses that are non-recurring and any expense that is not necessary for the ongoing operation of the business.

**Owner Earnings** – *See "SDCF" above.*

**Taxable Income** – *See "Pretax Profit."*

**Normalized Earnings** – "Normalized" refers to the act of adding back to profit all excess owner compensation (salaries that are not "fair market") and any expenses that are non-recurring or unnecessary for the ongoing operation of the business.

Now, you are at your country club and Jack Taylor tells you for the tenth time this year that he sold his company for 10 times profits. This time, to his surprise, you ask him what he means by "profits." After he gives you a flip answer such as "You know, the green stuff you put on the table in Vegas," you inquire as to what type of earnings he is referring to. He probably doesn't even know himself. But you will.

If he sold for 10 times his after-tax profit, then the price was $600,000. We see on the accompanying table that XYZ Co. reported Pretax Profit of $60,000. When we look at the income statement and footnotes, we see that adjusted seller's discretionary cash flow (SDCF) was $365,000. Consider this number and the definition of SDCF and you might come to believe that Jack Taylor didn't obtain the premium he boasts of.

We could estimate, assuming that 2001 was a typical year except for the lawsuit expense and assuming that his company was not a C-corporation and thereby subject to double taxation, that this company generates $300,000 in annual after-tax income to the owner. This is pre-debt service, so as long as the owner used leverage, his take-home would be less. Again, it does not appear that he sold for a premium.

In summary, the next time you hear a sale multiple you'll know that it tells us almost nothing unless we know the definition of profit used. Similarly, the sale price is almost meaningless unless you know the terms.

| **Year 2005 Income Statement XYZ Company** | |
|---|---|
| Revenue | $1,000 |
| Cost of Sales | ($300) |
| Gross Profit | $700 |
| Operating Expenses* | ($500) |
| Operating Profit | $200 |
| Non-Operating Expense** | ($100) |
| Pretax Profit | $100 |
| Tax | ($40) |
| After-Tax Profit | $60 |

* Operating Expenses include $100,000 of salary to the owner, $40,000 in owner perquisites and $25,000 in depreciation.

** Non-Operating Expense is $50,000 in interest and a $50,000 legal bill to settle a dispute.

| **Miscellaneous Profit Calculations**[1] | |
|---|---|
| Operating Profit | $200 |
| Pretax Profit | $100 |
| After-Tax Profit | $60 |
| EBIT | $150 |
| Adjusted EBIT[2] | $200 |
| EBITDA | $175 |
| Adjusted EBITADA[2] | $225 |
| SDCF[2] | $365 |

[1] For additional profit calculations, see each "profit" line on the accompanying XYZ income statement.

[2] Non-recurring expenses added back.

## SOMEDAY, A GOOD BUYER WILL COME ALONG.

*Was it patience that made you a success in business?*

"Shallow men believe in luck.
Strong men believe in cause and effect."

**Ralph Waldo Emerson**

# SECTION 10

## Value Drivers

Value drivers are characteristics that tend to enhance the value of private companies. Below are 17 key value drivers that enhance value because they reduce risk and lead to higher future profits. Business owners wishing to build the value of their business should focus on establishing the following characteristics in their businesses. Business sellers also should communicate to potential buyers the characteristics that exist in their businesses. The result will be higher sale prices.

**Operating Profits:** Business buyers buy businesses for the profits they can earn from them. The strongest indication of ability to generate profits is the historical performance. Higher profits lead to higher values. Consistency and stability of profits, over time, lead to higher values still. Profit margins exceeding industry averages will command even higher values.

**Revenue:** Although revenue does not equate to profits, it is a documented fact that higher revenue levels will lead to higher values or purchase prices for private companies. Even in a company not earning a profit, high revenue levels improve the likelihood that profits can be earned.

**Growth:** Growth of profits, and to a lesser degree growth in revenues, will command higher valuations. This is because buyers are concerned with the future much more than the past. Consistent growth, continued in the future, should lead to ever-increasing profits. Consequently, buyers will be willing to pay more for a growing business.

**Management and Employees:** The depth, quality, tenure, experience, success record and education of managers and key employees, such as salespersons, are all critical value drivers. Above-average human capital will reduce risk, improve the prospects for profitable performance and justify higher values.

**Niche, Market Position, Brand Awareness and Identity:** Companies will enjoy a higher value if they fill a definable niche and have strong brand awareness for their products and services.

**Multiple Markets:** Higher values can be justified if the product or service offerings have multiple markets or end users. This characteristic provides industry diversification, lower risk, added growth opportunities and higher values.

**Proprietary Products:** Your business will command a higher value if the products or services sold are one of a kind and their uniqueness can be protected. For example, a non-exclusive distributor enjoys little differentiation or protection from pricing pressure, whereas a manufacturer of a proprietary line of products should enjoy a more defensible market position (and higher profits).

**Customer Diversification, Loyalty and Financial Strength:** Diversification of customers will lead to higher values, as will customer loyalty and customer financial strength. The standard for diversification is 10 percent. If no single customer accounts for more than 10 percent of revenue, then the customer base is diverse.

**Product Mix and Gross Profit:** The greater the number of products the company sells and the greater the gross profit on each line, the stronger the case for a higher valuation.

**Condition and Appearance of Tangible Assets:** The assets of the business are needed to produce the product or service. Are they in a condition that will allow them to continue producing quality products efficiently and cost-effectively? Or are they worn and in need of repair or replacement?

**Replacement Value of Assets:** Viewing the business from the eyes of the buyer, how much money would it cost to duplicate the assets, infrastructure, personnel, systems and customers of the company? Don't forget to consider patents and other intangible assets such as favorable leases or agreements. Higher asset values lead to lower risk as they could be sold to return capital to the business owner if needed. Asset values could also be borrowed against them. Higher borrowing ability can lead to higher values because buyers can afford to pay higher prices.

**Interim Results:** Buyers are interested in what the business will do in the future. The best indication is the present. Strong current performance can justify higher price. A dip in performance always will put a drag on price.

**Growth Capacity:** If the existing employees, working capital, facilities and systems are adequate to support the projected growth over the next few years, a higher-than-average valuation will be supported.

**Projections:** The higher and more certain the projected sales and cash flow of the business, the higher the multiple of trailing cash flow.

**Contingent Risks:** Risk and uncertainty lower values. Value will decline if a company has existing or pending litigation, potential environmental issues, a seller that has a reputation for being litigious, is in a changing or threatened market niche or possesses other risk factors.

**Overall Reputation in the Community and Industry:** Healthy and favorable reputations make doing business easier – employees want to work for you, customers are more easily won, and vendors offer better service and terms. Is the company's reputation strong, or have they "burned bridges" and "worn out their welcome" within the community?

**Quality of Financial Information:** Financial statements present the financial health and performance of a company. The degree to which these reports may be relied upon to accurately reflect this will influence the price a buyer will be willing to pay. Audited financial statements by a well-known and independent audit firm are the highest-quality statements. Reviewed statements by the same would be the second preference.

## THE BUSINESS OWNER IS NO FOOL.

*A fool is as a fool does. Represent yourself and you'll have a fool for a client. Representation simply works. It works every day in our society – actors, athletes, lawyers and real estate agents. You want the best deal? Hire the best – an expert who is trained to get the best for you.*

**David L. Perkins, Jr.**

# SECTION 11

# Identifying the Value of a Business

After the various valuation methods are applied, a final value for the business can be estimated in a number of ways. First, if logic tells us that one of the methods used should offer a better representation of the true value of the business, the conclusion derived from that method should be used as the final conclusion.

For example, if the business is healthy and will be sold as a going concern and the income approach yields a higher value than the liquidation approach, then the conclusion derived from the liquidation approach should be ignored. Logic tells us that the business owner certainly would not sell for less than the going-concern value. But if the business is performing poorly and has a low value using the income methods, but the fixed assets have considerable value, the liquidation value would yield a higher value conclusion and would be selected. Why would the seller sell for less than the value of the underlying assets themselves?

If there are logical reasons that more than one valuation approach has merit, one could average the value conclusions to get the final estimate of value. Keep in mind, valuation is not an exact science – but part science and part art.

## What are the big mistakes made by do-it-yourself business sellers?

*We'll keep it to six:*

- *Waste time and money with buyers who will never close.*
- *No realistic understanding of fair value and terms.*
- *Naively negotiate directly with trained and experienced business buyers.*
- *Failure to control ego and emotion.*
- *Hire an attorney too soon.*
- *Poor salesmanship.*

**David L. Perkins, Jr.**

# SECTION 12

## Checking Value for Reasonableness (Method A)

A simple and very realistic method for checking a value conclusion for reasonableness is to estimate if the business will be able to pay off the debt service and provide a fair rate of return for the buyer, under some reasonable assumptions of deal structure. If the business being purchased will be operated, then this requires a projection of future cash flow. If the business will be liquidated, then all that is needed is to check the value.

To illustrate, let's assume that we estimated the value of XYZ Company to be $1,750,000. Does it pass a test of reasonableness? Well, let's first lay out the facts:

- We project annual pre-interest, pretax and pre-depreciation income to be $350,000.
- We expect to be able to borrow $1,000,000 from a bank, and we obtained this estimate from our pretax profit of $350,000 in year 1 and the income will grow at a constant rate of 10 percent per year thereafter.

We can use the formula for the Capitalized Future Income Method (CFIM) with a *constant growth rate*, an income approach described in Section 5 above. Let's also assume we determined that the appropriate discount rate for this investment is 30 percent. We value XYZ Company as follows:

$$PV = E1/(k-g)$$

*Where PV = Present Value*

*E1 = Expected Income in Year 1*

*k = Discount Rate*

*g = Annual Growth Rate of Expected Income*

$$PV = \$350{,}000/(.30 - .10)$$

$$= \$350{,}000/.20$$

$$= \$1{,}750{,}000$$

Is this value reasonable? Let's see.

**Test of Reasonableness #1:** Will the total purchase price equal cash flow assuming the entire price is financed (i.e., the buyer does not put any equity into the purchase)? This is not a realistic assumption because most lenders require the buyer invest equity into the deal. Nevertheless, this test determines whether the profits expected to be generated from the business are sufficient to pay back the borrowed money, plus interest, and pay a debt-rate of return to the buyer for his or her equity contributed.

To apply this to our example, the annual debt service (principal and interest) on $1,750,000 at a 9 percent annual rate (pick a market lending rate of interest) is $28,160 per month or $337,920 per year. This amount is less than the annual projected profits in year 1. Thus, our purchase price has met this simple test. Of course, in the interest of simplicity, taxes have been ignored. This may not be an unreasonable assumption because the interest portion of the debt service, which will be significant, will reduce the taxable income of the business, and the depreciation of the purchased assets, which also will be substantial. A detailed analysis of projected taxable income and taxes may be performed. But the goal of this publication is to keep the task as simple as possible, so we will not provide a more in-depth analysis herein.

Under this simple test, the rate of return on any equity contributed is quite low. Most investors in small and midsize private businesses would require a much higher rate of return, 25 percent or more. One mitigating factor here is the actual return to the equity interest will be higher than the 9 percent used when the pay-down of debt with each debt service payment is considered. A pay-down of debt is a form of return to the equity holders, as the equity of the business rises.

In addition, by assuming a seven-year amortization on the borrowing against the real estate, we have been conservative. Buyers of private businesses typically want the purchase debt to be amortized over a five-year period, or certainly no more than seven, but in our example real estate is included. It is likely a buyer could and would get longer-term financing on the real estate – probably 15 years – which would reduce the annual debt service requirement in our example.

Furthermore, the debt service coverage will be greater in year 2, and increasingly so in each successive year as our projected income rises each year by 10 percent.

**Test of Reasonableness #2:** How much money can be borrowed for the purchase? To answer this question, we apply the following commonly used borrowing rates to the balance sheet assets:

Accounts Receivable: 75 percent
Inventory: 50 percent
Fixed Assets: 50 percent
Real Estate: 80 percent

| | Year-End 2005 Adjusted | Borrowing Rate | Loanable Amount |
|---|---|---|---|
| Cash | $0 | N/A | |
| Receivables | $375 | 75% | $281 |
| Inventory | $350 | 50% | $175 |
| Other Current | $0 | | |
| Furniture, Fixtures and Equipment Net of Depreciation | $400 | 50% | $200 |
| Real Estate | $400 | 80% | $320 |
| Other Fixed Assets | $0 | | |
| **TOTAL BORROWED FUNDS** | | | **$976** |

We estimate $976,000 can be borrowed against the assets of the business and applied toward the purchase price of $1,750,000. Rounding this number to $975,000, a hypothetical buyer is left with $775,000 of the purchase price that must be found elsewhere. This can come from equity contributed by the buyer, financing provided by the seller, or both.

If a buyer can be found who is willing to put $775,000 in equity into the contemplated purchase, then no seller financing will be required and the total price of $1,750,000 can be paid. Buyers always want to keep their equity contribution to a minimum. Lower equity provides higher returns on equity through the principle of leverage. The equity contribution as a percentage of total purchase price is typically between 20 percent and 30 percent for small and midsize business purchases. Equity capital is scarce. Buyers of small and midsize businesses typically have limited capital (cash) to put into the purchase of a business. Therefore, as the required amount of equity rises, the number of capable buyers will fall sharply.

In our case, if the seller is unwilling to provide some financing, the buyer will be required to provide 44 percent of the total purchase price in equity if the $1.75 million purchase price is to be realized. This is very high. It is unlikely a buyer could be found who would be willing to do this. If we assume the maximum a buyer will contribute is 30 percent in equity, then a more reasonable purchase price for XYZ is $1,392,857, derived by dividing the borrowable funds of $975,000 by the percentage that can be financed with debt (70 percent). Because our income appears to be sufficient to service more debt, the seller may want to provide seller financing to enable the full price to be achieved. For each dollar the seller of XYZ is willing to finance, the purchase price should rise dollar for dollar up to the $1,750,000 price, approximately. The upper price threshold will be the highest price the buyer believes can be paid off with the projected profits. As is often the case, the seller has little disincentive to provide seller financing because he will have lost nothing if the buyer defaults on the note!

## TYPICALLY, SELLING A BUSINESS DOES NOT MAKE FINANCIAL SENSE.

---

*From an income standpoint, this is true. Private businesses are risky, volatile, and a real pain to manage. That's why they sell for just a few times their annual cash flow.*

*Let's say you sell for four times your annual earnings, thereby offering the buyer a 25 percent annual rate of return. You invest your sale proceeds in public stocks and bonds. Your income has declined substantially. The moral? Business owners sell primarily for non-financial reasons.*

**David L. Perkins, Jr.**

# SECTION 13

# Checking Purchase Price for Reasonableness (Method B)

When we estimate the value of a business, we are estimating the price at which it could be sold. Of course, buyers will buy a business only when it makes "financial sense" to do so. A purchase makes financial sense when the proposed price and terms allow for the following three tests to be met:

Test #1: Is the business able to pay fair compensation for the talent and labor contributed by each owner?

Test #2: Can all post-purchase debt be comfortably serviced by normal "commercial" terms?

Test #3: Will the equity holders receive a fair return on investment?

So XYZ Company is worth $1,200? Okay, let's see if it passes the three tests of reasonableness. To do this, you'll need:

a. *Beginning Balance Sheet*: Should be a "best guess" of what it will look like on the first day after the hypothetical purchase/sale before any purchase related debt or equity.

b. *Ten-Year Projections*: These must include annual income statements, balance sheets and statements of cash flows.

c. *Debt Service Requirements*: Projected until all purchase-related debt is repaid.

Below is the summary balance sheet and income statement for XYZ.

**XYZ Company**

| **Balance Sheet** | |
|---|---|
| Cash | $25 |
| Accounts Receivable | $300 |
| Inventory | $300 |
| Furniture, Fixtures and Equip. | $400 |
| **Total Assets** | **$1,025** |
| Accounts Payable | $100 |
| Other Current Liabilities | $50 |
| Long-Term Liabilities | $0 |
| Total Liabilities | $150 |
| Equity | $875 |
| **Total Debt and Equity** | **$1,025** |

| **Income Statement** | |
|---|---|
| Revenue | $2,500 |
| Cost of Goods Sold | ($1,500) |
| Gross Profit | $1,000 |
| Operating Expense | ($700) |
| Pretax Profit | $300 |
| Taxes | ($100) |
| Non-Cash Expense (Depreciation) | $50 |
| **Cash Flow (after tax)** | **$250** |

At the top of the table is the pro forma beginning balance sheet (day 1 of new ownership). Below it is a pro forma income statement and estimate of cash flow for the first year of ownership before any interest or principal payments on debt (purchase-related or otherwise). For simplicity, we will assume each year will perform as year 1 (i.e., flat income and cash flow in each year post-purchase).

**Test #1: Fair Compensation for the Talent and Labor of Each Owner-Employee?** Business owners are notorious for sacrificing pay. But why buy a business that cannot pay fair compensation to the owners for their talent, time and effort? What is "fair?" It's the compensation that could and would be obtained "on the open market." If you could get a job for $50,000 per year working full time, the business should be able to pay you this "fair market rate."

So the first test is, "Can the business afford to pay the working owners a fair price for their labor?" This test is met when, in your projections, you burden the business with fair compensation for all the owner/employees and the business will still make a profit and have positive cash flow from operations.

**Test #2: Will Projected Cash Flow Cover the Debt Service?** Businesses are purchased with debt and equity. The senior obligation is to debt. The second test of reasonableness is whether the business will generate enough cash to comfortably make all of its debt payment obligations – both interest and principal.

To estimate this, you need more than the price of the business. You need to know how the purchase price will be paid – the "deal structure." Because investors typically want to borrow as much as they are able (equity is scarce and more costly than debt), it makes sense to first estimate the amount of bank debt that could be borrowed against the assets of the business. To do this, take the pro forma balance sheet to your banker. Below we have applied common loan-to-value rules of thumb to XYZ's assets.

| | **Value** | **Loan to Value** | **Loan Amount** |
|---|---|---|---|
| Accounts Receivable | $300 | 80% | $240 |
| Inventory | $300 | 70% | $210 |
| Furniture, Fixtures and Equip. | $400 | 50% | $200 |
| **Total Bank Borrowing:** | | | **$650** |

As calculated, $650 can be borrowed against the assets of the business. Loan terms on business purchase transactions, non-real estate, are typically five to seven years. We'll use seven for our example and assume that the bank wants all of the debt repaid over the seven years (as opposed to leaving the A/R and inventory portion on a revolving line of credit) at a 7 percent rate.

The remainder ($550) of the total price must come from equity, seller financing or a blend of the two. Now every seller will say, "I won't seller-finance," but the numbers hardly ever work when there is no seller financing. And studies show that 80 percent of private businesses that sell do so with seller financing. (By the way, of the company's sales that do include seller financing, the most typical percentage of the price is 50 percent).

For this example, let's assume that the buyer and seller agree to split the balance of the purchase price that cannot be borrowed from a traditional lender. That places $275 in seller financing and $275 in cash contributed by the buyer (i.e., equity). So, the equity piece comes to 23 percent of the total purchase price. This is in the range of what we actually see in the real world (most deals have 20 percent to 30 percent).

Because the seller debt will be subordinate to the bank financing, it is more risky and merits a higher rate of interest than the senior debt. Let's say three points over prime or 9 percent.

Now, add to your projections the debt service obligations for both bank and seller financing, as in the accompanying table. For explanations of the other calculations in the table, study the notes.

| | Year 1 | Year 2 | Year 3 | Year 4 | Year 5 | Year 6 | Year 7 |
|---|---|---|---|---|---|---|---|
| Projected Cash Flow (after tax)[1] | 250 | 250 | 250 | 250 | 250 | 250 | 250 |
| Bank Loan Interest, Net of Tax[2] | $25 | $22 | $17 | $14 | $10 | $6 | $2 |
| Bank Loan Principal[3] | $93 | $93 | $93 | $93 | $93 | $93 | $93 |
| Seller Loan Interest, Net of Tax[4] | $14 | $11 | $10 | $7 | $5 | $3 | $1 |
| Seller Loan Principal[5] | $39 | $39 | $39 | $39 | $39 | $39 | $39 |
| Free Cash Flow[6] | $79 | $85 | $91 | $97 | $103 | $109 | $115* |
| Interest Expense Coverage[7] | 6.4 | 7.6 | 9.3 | 11.9 | 16.7 | 27.8 | 83.3 |
| Debt Service Coverage[8] | 1.5 | 1.5 | 1.6 | 1.6 | 1.7 | 1.8 | 1.9 |
| Internal Rate of Return (IRR) | 38% | n/a | n/a | n/a | n/a | n/a | n/a |

[1] Projected cash flow is derived by projections. Cash flow here is after tax and all expenses except purchase-related debt.

Notes continued on next page...

Continued from previous page.

[2] To keep our analysis on an after-tax cash basis, we adjust the interest expense to after tax. Doing so calls for a reduction of interest expense because interest is tax deductible, so the real cash cost of the interest is 60 percent of the gross or pretax cost (calculated by using a 40 percent blended federal and state tax rate). For example, bank loan interest expense in year one is $42, times 60 percent (calculated as one minus the tax rate of .40) is 25 percent.

[3] Annual bank loan principal is simply the borrowed amount ($650) divided by the loan term (seven years). No tax adjustment is needed because principal borrowing and repayment do not impact taxes.

[4] Seller loan interest is derived by using common terms for seller financing – seven-year note at prime-plus-3 percentage points (we used 9 percent). See note 2 above for the rationale for adjusting to after-tax.

[5] Seller loan principal is the annual amount of principal that must be paid on the seller note ($275 divided by 7).

[6] "Free cash flow" is the excess cash generated each year after all obligations are met (compensation, taxes, interest and principal). This is the number that contributes to the investor's (buyer's) return on investment (calculated in this case by the IRR method).

[7] Interest coverage ratio is an important indicator of the ease with which cash flow is able to pay interest burden. Banks, in the very worst case, want to be sure interest can be paid. The coverage here is very healthy.

[8] Debt service coverage ratio shows the ease with which the business is able to meet its total principal and interest obligations. A ratio of 1.0 would indicate that there is just enough cash to meet the P&I burden. Lenders and investors want a cushion for safety, of course. 1.5 is a common threshold of safety. Anything above 1.5 is even healthier. As we can see, debt service coverage begins at a fairly healthy 1.5 and then slowly improves in the later years.

* Beginning in year 8, free cash flow is $250, because all debt service will be paid by end of year 7. This is also after fair compensation to the owners.

**Test #3: Will the equity holders receive a fair return on investment?** Well, what is a "fair return" for an equity investment in a private company? We know that over the past 80 years in the United States, holders of equity in publicly traded companies have earned per year, on average, 11 percent and 18 percent for large-cap and micro-cap stocks, respectively. Given that equity stakes in private companies tend to be much more risky, slower growth, volatile and illiquid, return on investment should be higher. Generally, private equity stakes should yield AT LEAST 25 percent, if not higher.

So, what do we estimate the return to equity would be on XYZ Company at the $1,200 valuation and using the deal structure example above? Using your financial calculator or Excel, you can take the projected annual free cash flow from the table above, apply it to the initial cash invested ($275) and you will get a 38 percent after-tax internal rate of return. This substantially exceeds our minimum threshold of 25 percent, so the estimated value of XYZ of $1,200 meets the third test.

*This article is adapted from an article titled "The Justification of Purchase Test" by Rand M. Curtiss, which appeared in the fall 1999 issue of* Business Appraisal Practice.

*Note: In an attempt to keep this example simple, some liberties have been taken. Before you make investment decisions, consult an expert.*

## IN A SMALL COMPANY, EVERYBODY MUST BE SELLING ALL THE TIME.

---

*Selling is honorable work – particularly in a startup where it's the difference between life and death. And make sure that the group has a sense of humor. You're going to be spending a lot of time living together as a team.*

**John Doerr*, Kleiner Perkins Caufield & Byers**

**arguably the most influential venture capitalist of the past 25 years, who funded startups such as Sun Microsystems, Compaq, Lotus, Intuit, Netscape and Amazon*

# SECTION 14

## *The Minority Shareholder:* What You Have and Don't Have

Minority shareholders of private companies have little power and control in most cases. The actual rights and powers of the minority shareholder are described in the documents that govern the particular organization–such as the articles of incorporation or operating agreement. But in most cases, a majority of shares will win votes and, therefore, control the company. The controlling shareholder or shareholders will have the power to appoint who manages the business, how it is managed and how much the managers and employees are paid. The controlling shareholder has broad freedom to set his or her own salary and perquisites, and if or when to distribute profits to shareholders. When this is paired with the understanding that the value of an ownership interest in a business is a function of the certainty with which income will be received, the lack of control as to whether profits or cash will be returned to the owner has a significant dampening affect on the value of minority interests. For this reason, minority interests in private companies typically trade at a significant discount to control positions. In fact, discounts of

25 percent to well over 50 percent are common. The exact value of minority interest is a function of the particular characteristics of the particular situation.

Characteristics that enhance the value of minority positions include:

**Dispersal of Ownership Interests:** If a single shareholder controls a majority of shares, then the minority discount typically would be larger. If there are many shareholders and no controlling shareholder, the minority shareholder, by aligning with other minority shareholders, could garner a control block. This would potentially create a milder minority discount.

**Shareholder Agreements or Operating Agreements:** If the governing documents of the organization provide meaningful rights and protections to the minority shareholder, lower discounts may be merited.

**Put Options:** If the company has any obligation to buy back stockholder shares under certain circumstances, this could reduce the minority discount, depending on the terms and the likelihood of occurrence.

**Historical Treatment of Minority Shareholders:** If shareholders historically have been treated fairly and have been paid fair value for their interests by controlling shareholders or the company, then lower discounts could be merited.

**Laws:** Some states have stronger protections for minority shareholders. If the company is organized in a state with such protections, discounts will tend to be lower.

When we value a company as explained in this report, we are valuing the equity of the business. This means 100 percent of the ownership interest. If a company is valued at $1,000,000 and there are 100 shares outstanding, then each share is worth $10,000. What would a buyer pay for 25 percent of this company? A buyer probably could not be found at almost any price because he or she likely would endure significant uncertainty as to whether income would be received or the shares could ever be liquidated (sold).

Most of the value of the typical private company is in the first 50.01 percent interest, assuming the governing documents call for majority rule. To the extent that a minority interest reasonably can expect to generate income in the future, the anticipated future income can be valued as described in this publication – as a function of the amount of anticipated income, the timing of receipt of such income, the time value of money and the risk or certainty with which such income could be expected to be received.

If you are a minority shareholder, don't feel helpless. You do have rights. Investigate the laws in your state and your rights under the documents that govern the management of your company. Know your rights and exercise those rights to garner the most for your ownership. For many minority shareholders, the "nuisance factor" may be their most significant leverage in negotiating a sale of shares to the controlling owner or owners.

**SECTION 15**

# Private Company Values vs. Public Company Values

The mistake of comparing large public companies to smaller private companies is made quite frequently. In fact, the two have little in common. Consider the following differences between public and private companies:

| | **Public Company** | **Private Company** |
|---|---|---|
| Revenues | Typically very large | Typically small |
| Asset Values | Typically very large | Typically lower |
| Growth Rates | Typically higher | Typically low |
| Access to Additional Capital | Very good | Generally poor |
| Ability to Attract Top Talent | Excellent | Poor |
| Liquidity of Ownership Interest | Excellent | Very poor |

Characteristics such as those listed above impact value significantly. Each of the characteristics above tends to lower the risk inherent in investments in publicly traded companies and heighten the risk inherent in private companies. The values paid for shares of public companies are typically much higher than private companies.

For the reasons described herein, there is little merit to valuing a private company by comparing it to a publicly traded company.

# Section 16

## About Your Money

Your money is yours. You can do with it as you wish. But when it comes to investing, I suggest you heed the advice of Benjamin Graham – arguably the greatest investment philosopher of all time. He brought structure and logic to the business of security analysis – that is, the discipline of investing in companies by their common stock (i.e., equity) and, to a lesser extent, their debt securities (i.e., bonds). He is credited with founding the discipline of value investing, which is the process of identifying and investing in undervalued equity interests. He was also teacher and mentor to the most successful investor of all time – Warren Buffett. Buffett explains that his secret to investing is simple – follow the advice of Ben Graham.

To the astounding benefit of you and me, Graham personally outlined his investment philosophy in *The Intelligent Investor*. It is written, as he says, "for the laymen" and is well within the intellectual reach of common folks like you and me.

What advice does Graham have for owners, and buyers, of private businesses? Well, Graham and Buffett primarily invest in publicly traded companies, but they also invest in private companies. And they will tell you that there's no difference in analyzing a private company vs. a public one. In fact, they explain that most buyers of publicly traded stocks err in that they focus their analysis (that is, if they do any at all) on the stock itself rather than the company in which they are buying an interest.

To the contrary, Graham and Buffett urge investors to analyze prospective investments as if they were buying the entire company. After all, whether you are buying an equity interest that accounts for a small fraction of ownership, or 100 percent, you are still betting on the future performance of the company (if you are applying Graham's methods).

True investing is not simply "watching stocks go up and down and jumping in when you think it's about to go up." Graham's philosophy is disciplined: buy interests in companies (as opposed to myopically buying shares of stock); do so only under certain, very special circumstances; and hold the position long-term.

Here are some other themes in *The Intelligent Investor*:

<u>Investing is not "trading in the market"</u>: Trading based on analytics and/or technical or trend analysis employs methodologies that are in stark contrast to sound business sense. It is unlikely to lead to lasting success (in investing).

<u>Defensive Investor</u>: If the proceeds of investing will be used to live, retire or serve some other important purpose, then the only logical approach is one that ensures safety.

Keep it simple: Buy only at a price that is very safe. Buy only very high-quality and stable companies with outstanding, stable management. Stay diversified (10 to 15 investments). Hold each investment as long as you logically expect the business (as opposed to the stock) to continue to perform well.

Nobody can predict the future: Not you; not "Wall Street Experts." So don't try, and don't rely on the predictions of others. Be a defensive investor, stick to the keep-it-simple suggestions, and include an ample "margin of error."

Buy companies, not stocks: This way, you'll focus on the intrinsic value of a company – the real stuff that underpins the value of a stock. That is, value based on the balance sheet and income-generating performance of the company rather than an arbitrary stock price.

Margin of safety: Absolutely essential in investing. You must not lose principal, so the only prudent thing to do is invest only when there is a healthy margin of safety. In other words, even if your analysis is flawed or the business has some unforeseen problems (and it will), you will not be at risk of losing your investment.

Investing is not gambling or speculation: Investments are endeavors that hold promise, based on solid and thorough analysis, of safety of principal and an adequate return. Endeavors that don't meet these criteria are speculative.

Be willing to be different: To obtain a return higher than the average, you must be different. Follow the masses (even the "Wall Street Experts") and you'll get the results of the masses (poor ones).

Buffett says, "If you follow the behavioral and business principles that Graham advocates, and if you pay special attention to the invaluable advice in Chapters 8 and 20, you will not get a poor result..."

The strategy outlined in Graham's *The Intelligent Investor* is fairly simple and easy to understand. It IS within the reach of most of us who have some education and experience in business, finance, accounting and investments. If you are looking for a sound investment strategy or a means for analyzing a purchase of stock in any company, here are suggestions from the man who mentored the "Oracle of Omaha" – the wealthiest man on the planet (literally) – who built his wealth simply doing what this book, and his teacher, says. What more do you want?

IF THE PROCEEDS OF INVESTING WILL BE USED TO LIVE, RETIRE OR SERVE SOME OTHER IMPORTANT PURPOSE, THEN THE ONLY LOGICAL APPROACH IS ONE THAT ENSURES SAFETY.

# Glossary of Terms

**Adjusted Book Value** – (1) The value of an asset or liability after adjustments have been made to its balance sheet value. (2) The equity value of a business after adjustments have been made to the book value of assets and/or liabilities of the business. Such adjustments typically are made to more accurately reflect current market values of the assets, liabilities or equity of the company.

**Appraisal** – *See Valuation.*

**Balance Sheet** – A part of a company's financial statements, the balance sheet simply lists the assets and liabilities of a company. Customary practice is to list the assets above the liabilities, then present the difference – referring to the differences as the equity or net worth of the business.

**Blue Sky** – *See Goodwill.*

**Book Value** – The value of an asset, liability or equity account as per the financial statements of the business.

**Capitalization** – The total amount of all long-term capital in a business, also referred to as Total Capitalization.

**Capitalization of Earnings** – The conversion of an income stream into value.

**Capitalization Rate** – Any divisor used to convert an income stream to value. Capitalization rates can be estimated, determined or calculated. *See Section 5, Income Approach.*

**Comparable Sales Method** – A Market Approach method of valuation that estimates value by using data from sale of other comparable goods, ownership rights or businesses and comparing the data to what is being valued. *See Section 5, Market Approach.*

**Cost of Capital** – The rate of return the market requires to attract funds to a particular investment. Also, the return on equity required by a particular investor. The cost of capital will have two components – time value of money and risk.

**Depreciation** – The steady decline in the value of an asset over time. In accounting, depreciation is the dollar amount by which the value of an asset has been reduced on the balance sheet since its original purchase.

**Discount** – A reduction in value or the act of reducing value.

**Discount Rate** – The rate at which dollars expected to be received in the future are discounted to calculate their value today. Represents the required rate of return or cost of capital. *See Section 4.*

**Discount for Lack of Control** – An amount or percentage deducted from the value of an asset or business that is meant to compensate the owner for uncertainty associated with a lack of some or all of the powers of control. *See Section 13.*

**Discount for Lack of Marketability** – An amount or percentage deducted from the value of an asset or business that is meant to compensate the owner for risk associated with uncertainty as to the ease with which it may be turning into cash, when desired. *See Section 14.*

**Fair Market Value** – The price at which property would change hands between a hypothetical willing and able buyer and a hypothetical willing and able seller, acting at arm's length in an open and unrestricted market, when neither is under any compulsion to buy or sell and both have reasonable knowledge of the relevant facts. *See Sections 4 and 5.*

**Future Value** – The value of a dollar or dollars received at a future date.

**Generally Accepted Accounting Standards (GAAP)** – The set of rules for accounting that are set forth in the pronouncements of the Financial Accounting Standards Board (FASB).

**Going Concern** – An ongoing operating business enterprise.

**Going-Concern Value** – The value of a business or enterprise that is expected to continue to operate in the future.

**Goodwill** – The intangible asset that may arise or exist in a business enterprise as a result of the name, reputation, competency, location, product, service, customer lists, etc. Such value, when it exists, is separate and distinct from the tangible assets of a business enterprise. *See Section 4.*

**Goodwill Value** – The value attributable to Goodwill, as differentiated from the value attributable to the tangible assets of the business.

**Hurdle Rate** – *See Discount Rate.*

**Income Approach** – A method for calculating value that converts anticipated profits or cash flow into a present value dollar amount. *See Section 5.*

**Investment Value** – The value a business has to a particular investor based on individual investment requirements and expectations. *See Section 3.*

**Invested Capital** – The sum of long-term debt and equity invested in a business. *See also Capitalization and Total Capitalization.*

**Intangible Assets** – Assets that cannot be physically touched, seen or felt. Common intangible assets are goodwill, copyrights, patents, royalty rights and contracts.

**Lack-of-Control Discount** – *See Discount for Lack of Control.*

**Liquidity** – The ability of a company to pay its debt obligations as they come due.

**Liquidation or Liquidation Value** – The amount of net cash obtained by selling the assets of a business piecemeal (not as a going concern). *See Section 5.*

**Long-Term Capital** – *See Invested Capital.*

**Market Approach** – A method for valuing an asset or business that compares the subject asset or company to similar ones that have been sold. *See Section 5.*

**Market Value** – *See Fair Market Value.*

**Marketability** – The ability to quickly convert an asset to cash with minimal cost. *See Section 4.*

**Marketability Discount** – *See Discount for Lack of Marketability.*

**Net Book Value** – The value of an asset on a balance sheet net of any depreciation recorded against such asset on the balance sheet. Also, the difference between the net book value of assets and liabilities on a balance sheet.

**Net Worth** – Assets minus liabilities. Found on the bottom of a balance sheet. Also referred to as Book Value and Equity.

**Opportunity Cost of Capital** – *See Discount Rate.*

**Present Value** – The value of a good, service or benefit represented in dollars today. *See Section 4.*

**Price-Earnings Multiple** – The ratio between the market value of a company's stock and the annual earnings of the company. Commonly used to analyze the pricing of shares of publicly traded stock, the price-earnings multiple is stated on a per-share basis with the price per share as the numerator and the per-share earnings as the denominator. For example: If a share of Pepsi® stock trades for $10 and the annual earnings per share are $1, the P/E is 10. Or, if for whatever reason we establish a particular private company is worth five times its earnings, and it earns $150,000 per year, a value of $750,000 could be calculated.

**Replacement Value** – The company's assets are valued as if they had been purchased in today's market. With past inflation, the replacement value generally exceeds a company's reported net book value. *See Section 5.*

**Risk** – Degree of uncertainty as to the realization of expected future returns. *See Section 4.*

**Risk-Free Rate** – The rate of return available in the marketplace on an investment free of collection or default risk. *See Section 4.*

**Seller Financing** – A loan made by a business seller to the buyer of his or her business. *See Section 12.*

**Synergistic Buyer** – A buyer who possesses certain qualities, characteristics or attributes that – when combined with a particular business – might allow it to earn financial returns exceeding what would otherwise be possible. *See Section 4.*

**Tangible Assets** – Assets that can be physically seen, touched or felt. Those assets carried on a company's balance sheet that has a specific (or realizable) value and are physical or material in nature. Common intangible assets are cash, receivables, inventory, equipment, land and buildings.

**Tangible Book Value** – The value of a business, as per the balance sheet of the business, after eliminating any intangible assets such as goodwill or capitalized startup costs. *See also: Tangible Assets.*

**Terms** – The portion of a business sale price to be paid by the buyer to the seller after closing and subject to the occurrence of certain events.

**Time Value of Money** – The concept that a dollar today is worth more than a dollar in the future. *See Discount Rate and Section 4.*

**Total Capitalization** – *See Invested Capital.*

**Valuation** – The process of assigning a specific dollar value to something. This term is used synonymously with appraisal herein.

**Value** – Worth or utility derived from a good or service by its owner or contemplated owner.

# Present Value Table

PresentValue of $1(PVIF)

P = S(1+r)-N

| | 1% | 2% | 3% | 4% | 5% | 6% | 7% | 8% | 9% | 10% | 11% | 12% | 13% | 14% | 15% | 20% | 30% | 40% | 50% |
|---|---|---|---|---|---|---|---|---|---|---|---|---|---|---|---|---|---|---|---|
| **1** | 0.990 | 0.980 | 0.971 | 0.962 | 0.952 | 0.943 | 0.935 | 0.926 | 0.917 | 0.909 | 0.901 | 0.893 | 0.885 | 0.877 | 0.870 | 0.833 | 0.769 | 0.714 | 0.667 |
| **2** | 0.980 | 0.961 | 0.943 | 0.925 | 0.907 | 0.890 | 0.873 | 0.857 | 0.842 | 0.826 | 0.812 | 0.797 | 0.783 | 0.769 | 0.756 | 0.694 | 0.592 | 0.510 | 0.444 |
| **3** | 0.971 | 0.942 | 0.915 | 0.889 | 0.864 | 0.840 | 0.816 | 0.794 | 0.772 | 0.751 | 0.731 | 0.712 | 0.693 | 0.675 | 0.658 | 0.579 | 0.455 | 0.364 | 0.296 |
| **4** | 0.961 | 0.924 | 0.888 | 0.855 | 0.823 | 0.792 | 0.763 | 0.735 | 0.708 | 0.683 | 0.659 | 0.636 | 0.613 | 0.592 | 0.572 | 0.482 | 0.350 | 0.260 | 0.198 |
| **5** | 0.951 | 0.906 | 0.863 | 0.822 | 0.784 | 0.747 | 0.713 | 0.681 | 0.650 | 0.621 | 0.593 | 0.567 | 0.543 | 0.519 | 0.497 | 0.402 | 0.269 | 0.186 | 0.132 |
| **6** | 0.942 | 0.888 | 0.837 | 0.790 | 0.746 | 0.705 | 0.666 | 0.630 | 0.596 | 0.564 | 0.535 | 0.507 | 0.480 | 0.456 | 0.432 | 0.335 | 0.207 | 0.133 | 0.088 |
| **7** | 0.933 | 0.871 | 0.813 | 0.760 | 0.711 | 0.665 | 0.623 | 0.583 | 0.547 | 0.513 | 0.482 | 0.452 | 0.425 | 0.400 | 0.376 | 0.279 | 0.159 | 0.095 | 0.059 |
| **8** | 0.923 | 0.853 | 0.789 | 0.731 | 0.677 | 0.627 | 0.582 | 0.540 | 0.502 | 0.467 | 0.434 | 0.404 | 0.376 | 0.351 | 0.327 | 0.233 | 0.123 | 0.068 | 0.039 |
| **9** | 0.914 | 0.837 | 0.766 | 0.703 | 0.645 | 0.592 | 0.544 | 0.500 | 0.460 | 0.424 | 0.391 | 0.361 | 0.333 | 0.308 | 0.284 | 0.194 | 0.094 | 0.048 | 0.026 |
| **10** | 0.905 | 0.820 | 0.744 | 0.676 | 0.614 | 0.558 | 0.508 | 0.463 | 0.422 | 0.386 | 0.352 | 0.322 | 0.295 | 0.270 | 0.247 | 0.162 | 0.073 | 0.035 | 0.017 |
| **11** | 0.896 | 0.804 | 0.722 | 0.650 | 0.585 | 0.527 | 0.475 | 0.429 | 0.388 | 0.350 | 0.317 | 0.287 | 0.261 | 0.237 | 0.215 | 0.135 | 0.056 | 0.025 | 0.012 |
| **12** | 0.887 | 0.788 | 0.701 | 0.625 | 0.557 | 0.497 | 0.444 | 0.397 | 0.356 | 0.319 | 0.286 | 0.257 | 0.231 | 0.208 | 0.187 | 0.112 | 0.043 | 0.018 | 0.008 |
| **13** | 0.879 | 0.773 | 0.681 | 0.601 | 0.530 | 0.469 | 0.415 | 0.368 | 0.326 | 0.290 | 0.258 | 0.229 | 0.204 | 0.182 | 0.163 | 0.093 | 0.033 | 0.013 | 0.005 |
| **14** | 0.870 | 0.758 | 0.661 | 0.577 | 0.505 | 0.442 | 0.388 | 0.340 | 0.299 | 0.263 | 0.232 | 0.205 | 0.181 | 0.160 | 0.141 | 0.078 | 0.025 | 0.009 | 0.003 |
| **15** | 0.861 | 0.743 | 0.642 | 0.555 | 0.481 | 0.417 | 0.362 | 0.315 | 0.275 | 0.239 | 0.209 | 0.183 | 0.160 | 0.140 | 0.123 | 0.065 | 0.020 | 0.006 | 0.002 |
| **16** | 0.853 | 0.728 | 0.623 | 0.534 | 0.458 | 0.394 | 0.339 | 0.292 | 0.252 | 0.218 | 0.188 | 0.163 | 0.141 | 0.123 | 0.107 | 0.054 | 0.015 | 0.005 | 0.002 |
| **17** | 0.844 | 0.714 | 0.605 | 0.513 | 0.436 | 0.371 | 0.317 | 0.270 | 0.231 | 0.198 | 0.170 | 0.146 | 0.125 | 0.108 | 0.093 | 0.045 | 0.012 | 0.003 | 0.001 |
| **18** | 0.836 | 0.700 | 0.587 | 0.494 | 0.416 | 0.350 | 0.296 | 0.250 | 0.212 | 0.180 | 0.153 | 0.130 | 0.111 | 0.095 | 0.081 | 0.038 | 0.009 | 0.002 | 0.001 |
| **19** | 0.828 | 0.686 | 0.570 | 0.475 | 0.396 | 0.331 | 0.277 | 0.232 | 0.194 | 0.164 | 0.138 | 0.116 | 0.098 | 0.083 | 0.070 | 0.031 | 0.007 | 0.002 | 0.000 |
| **20** | 0.820 | 0.673 | 0.554 | 0.456 | 0.377 | 0.312 | 0.258 | 0.215 | 0.178 | 0.149 | 0.124 | 0.104 | 0.087 | 0.073 | 0.061 | 0.026 | 0.005 | 0.001 | 0.000 |
| **25** | 0.780 | 0.610 | 0.478 | 0.375 | 0.295 | 0.233 | 0.184 | 0.146 | 0.116 | 0.092 | 0.074 | 0.059 | 0.047 | 0.038 | 0.030 | 0.010 | 0.001 | 0.000 | 0.000 |
| **30** | 0.742 | 0.552 | 0.412 | 0.308 | 0.231 | 0.174 | 0.131 | 0.099 | 0.075 | 0.057 | 0.044 | 0.033 | 0.026 | 0.020 | 0.015 | 0.004 | 0.000 | 0.000 | 0.000 |